RECENT DOONESBURY BOOKS BY G.B. TRUDEAU

Read My Lips, Make My Day, Eat Quiche and Die!
Give Those Nymphs Some Hooters!
You're Smokin' Now, Mr. Butts!
I'd Go With the Helmet, Ray
Welcome to Club Scud!
What Is It, Tink, Is Pan in Trouble?
Quality Time on Highway 1
Washed Out Bridges and Other Disasters
In Search of Cigarette Holder Man
Doonesbury Nation

IN LARGE FORMAT

The Doonesbury Chronicles
Doonesbury's Greatest Hits
The People's Doonesbury
Doonesbury Dossier: The Reagan Years
Doonesbury Deluxe: Selected Glances Askance
Recycled Doonesbury: Second Thoughts on a Gilded Age
Action Figure!
The Portable Doonesbury

TWENTY-FIVE YEARS OF DOONESBURY

G.B. Trudeau

Andrews and McMeel
A Universal Press Syndicate Company
Kansas City

DOONESBURY is distributed internationally by Universal Press Syndicate.

Flashbacks: Twenty-Five Years of Doonesbury copyright ©1995 by G.B. Trudeau. All rights reserved. Printed in the United States of America. No part of this book may be used or reproduced in any manner whatsoever without written permission except in the case of reprints in the context of reviews. For information, write Andrews and McMeel, a Universal Press Syndicate Company, 4900 Main Street, Kansas City, Missouri 64112.

Library of Congress Catalog Card Number: 95-77566

ISBN: 0-8362-0436-0 (paperback)
      0-8362-0437-9 (hardback)

Design by Jessica Helfand and Melissa Tardiff, the Jessica Helfand Studio

THIS BOOK IS DEDICATED TO JANE —
WIFE, FRIEND, MOVIE COMPANION,
TAKE-OUT SPECIALIST,
AND ALL-AROUND FABULOUS BABE

A Few Words from the Author

AT SOME unspecified point in mid-life, one suddenly starts paying closer attention to compliments, holding on to them as if each might be the last. "What a nice hat," for instance, becomes as valued as, "Great merger, guy!" In evolutionary terms, this is a significant advance from the sense of fraudulence that attends even the faintest praise for the tiny triumphs of youth. Once well beyond the possibility of wunderkindom, with options closing behind you with the finality of steel doors, it becomes necessary to find in kind words some hint that you've lived your life to good purpose — or failing that, to maximum effect.

Maximum effect has always been my fallback position. I know what a life of good purpose is — there were plenty in my family who embodied it — but I chose, I believe, the tougher route. I say tougher, because anyone can be beloved. Well, not anyone, but if you're willing to set aside fifty years of your life to the service of others, it can be done. Far more difficult is *not* leading the communitarian, civic-minded life, but somehow seeming *of* it. This is the lie that people in daily journalism live. In the case of the political cartoonist, it's a lie that people generally see through.

A favorite cartoon panel of mine, done some years ago by the late B. Kliban, showed a cartoonist walking down the street, resplendent in ascot and smoking jacket, undraped women draped on either arm, with a policeman clearing the sidewalk of the common rabble before him. As the officer sends a hapless pedestrian sprawling into traffic, he bellows, "Get out of the way, you swine — a cartoonist is coming!"

The joke, of course, depends entirely on the common understanding that society accords the cartoonist no respect whatsoever. Indeed, it is not unusual for a reader to approach me with the following approbation: "I so enjoy your . . . your . . . column." This is invariably followed by an expression of relief that he or she has managed to convey admiration for my work while sparing us both the embarrassment of actually naming it.

Why does the centuries-old art of satiric drawing invite such scorn? Well, partly because it richly deserves it. It comes by its vulgarity quite honestly, requiring a broad, popular audience to survive. Just ask any syndicated European cartoonist, of which there are none. What the beaux-arts world knows but can't admit is that pandering is a lot harder than its working definition seems to imply. If this were not so, everyone would be rich and famous and there'd be no one left to apply for NEA grants.

The other reason that my craft is held in such low regard, I think, has to do with its ephemeral nature. Who reads yesterday's papers? The cartoonist's targets — picked off from the passing parade — are usually quickly forgotten in the larger sweep of history. All the more reason, of course, that villains should be laid low with dispatch; ridicule must be timely if it is to be socially useful. There is a genteel school of satire that holds that the practitioner should spare the individual and attack the larger vice. Such satirists are more correctly called humorists, as they usually have nothing more in mind than to plumb public sentiment for a good laugh. There is a certain kind of joke — the good-natured, Will Rogers-style put-down of politicians for their hypocrisy or lawyers for their greed — that is at heart profoundly cynical, because categorical attacks leave no room for hope.

This explains, I suppose, my personal taste for the ad hominem. I prefer to attack a Dan Rostenkowski or a Johnny Cochran in the specific, because such satire implies — or should — that there are moral choices in life, that not everyone behaves this way, and with reason.

Mort Sahl tells the story of visiting a writer on the set of *Saturday Night Live* during its early, headier days. A skit about Henry Kissinger had been scheduled, so Sahl, who kept voluminous files about the Secretary of State, coyly asked the writer why he was attacking Kissinger. "Because he's in charge," came the self-satisfied reply. That was all. Nothing about Vietnam. Or Chile. Not a word about the criminal bombing of Cambodia. The motivation was nothing more than the banal, adolescent need to strike at someone in authority.

Now this is profitable work if you can get it, and you usually can, since scorched-earth humor took off soon thereafter — spreading its spawn across the breadth of the entertainment industry. But it did seem to Sahl — and to me — a lost opportunity, that it was a pity that so much of this smart, caustic, irony-driven satire didn't aim higher, didn't even try to illuminate. Moreover, the humorist without humility, floating above it all, misses the fattest target of them all — himself. It's a target that the greats — Mark Twain, Woody Allen, Jules Feiffer — never took their eyes off of. When Walt Kelly wrote that we have met the enemy and he may be us, he was telling us that the human comedy is all-inclusive, that we're all in the same leaky boat together.

This is why *Doonesbury* is populated by other characters besides the politicians. I need proxies, loyal representatives of my own sovereign state of confusion. As Steve Martin says, comedy isn't pretty. Twenty-five years into it, I'm still trying to get it right. The strip remains a work in progress, an imperfect chronicle of human imperfection.

There are many who cannot escape their share of responsibility in this enterprise, and to all I extend my profound thanks. Among them are my wife, Jane; my inking assistant and friend of 24 years, Don Carlton; my trusty sounding board and book editor, David Stanford; my long-time strip editor and human firewall, Lee Salem; Mike Seeley, who runs the office with gracious efficiency; and, of course, Kathy Andrews and my large family of friends and colleagues at Universal Press Syndicate. If I fail to include my boss, John McMeel, it is only for the best of reasons: We are in the middle of contract negotiations.

Garry Trudeau
October 18, 1995

1970~1974

"Yes, dammit.
I'm the model for Michael."

—GARRY TRUDEAU, 1971

bull tales

WELL, I LET YOU GUYS TAKE THE LAST PLAY AND WHAT HAPPENED? YOU BUTCHERED IT! YOUR BIG CHANCE FOR YOU / ALL TO MAKE IT WITHOUT ME AND YOU BLEW IT.

"The lively exchange between Brian Dowling and Cal Hill was another in the daily accounts of the Yale football team as portrayed through the pen of Garry Trudeau, a student, in his popular *Peanuts*-style comic strip in *the Yale Daily News*, the student newspaper."
—*The New York Times, November 20, 1968*

"G.B. Trudeau never made a diving catch in the end zone with 30 seconds to go, but he thought about it a lot."

—NEW HAVEN REGISTER, MARCH 1, 1970

Bull Tales, by G.B. Trudeau, first appears in *Yale Daily News* and within a few weeks attracts the attention of Universal Press Syndicate co-founder and editor, James F. Andrews.

Trudeau's other passion: third-string intramural hockey.

HAPPY
HALLOWEEN
YOURSELF!

Renamed after its principal
character, *Doonesbury*
debuts in 28 newspapers.

Q .... Fluke start, right?

A .... Pretty much. I was approached about syndication during my junior year in college, after an arduous four-week apprenticeship on the school paper. Incredibly, the offer didn't strike me as particularly remarkable. It was the very essence of being in the right place at the right time, but when you're young, you don't understand serendipity. You feel entitled, even to your accidents.

—FRANCIS B. TRUDEAU
to his son, Garry, 1971

Trudeau makes the first of the only two television appearances of his career, on "To Tell the Truth." Three of the four panelists fail to correctly guess his identity; Trudeau wins $167 and a pair of cuff links.

Comic strip fame brought costume jewelry.

Doonesbury escapes cancellation in a *Macon Telegraph* readers' referendum. For *Doonesbury*, 27; against, 22. It is the first of many such polls taken around the country.

ASK THE GLOBE

Q— I really wish you would print a picture of Garry Trudeau who draws the fantastic *Doonesbury* cartoon. Those people are super cool.—*L.E., Saugus*

A—Here's super cool Trudeau.

—*The Boston Globe, 1972*

The post-surgeon-general Belmondo pose was soon withdrawn.

—ART BUCHWALD

A legacy terrorist: Phred's father had
harassed the French

25

Q .... You got caught up in feminism pretty early, didn't you?

A .... Yes, in early 1970, only seven months after Gloria Steinem reportedly signed on. Seven months is 14 years in pig time. I found that out when I moved to a ski resort, where the locals were a full generation away from getting it. Whenever I brought up the subject, people would dive through the windows. Even the women shunned me, which was pitiful, because the whole point, of course, was to get dates.

First stop, Cleveland.

"A woman friend told me all about someone named Joanie Caucus. I sat through the conversation smiling patiently, humoring my friend, because I did not believe her. Joanie Caucus, she told me, was funny. It seemed to me that the likelihood of that was next to impossible."
— *Nora Ephron*

A Sunday strip about Zonker, kids, and hashish brings down a firestorm of criticism. One Texas editor is awakened by an irate minister on his doorstep early in the morning.

" I also had threats from Abilene and Paris, Texas.… Paris even ran a letter of apology to their readers and said they would refuse to deliver the entire section if it happened again. I think the thing that disturbed most of the publishers is that professional school administrators were the leaders of the protests."

—*Charles O. Kilpatrick, Editor,*
San Antonio News,
in a letter to UPS president
John McMeel

Q .... The hashish strip. What was the deal there?

A .... I'm not sure. I was 24. It was 1972. Someone once asked Robert Crumb why he drew his infamous incest cartoon. He replied, "I think I was just being a punk." There may have been some of that.

May 10 **1973**

The unanticipated resignation of Watergate conspirator John Ehrlichman causes the recall of a week of strips.

—JOHN EHRLICHMAN
in a letter to Trudeau

May 20 **1973**

The Washington Post tells its readers, "If anyone is going to find any defendant guilty, it's going to be the due process of justice, not a comic strip artist." The editor of *The Boston Globe* gives a $50 bonus to the copy editor who flagged the offending strip, explaining, "There are bold graphics involved."

Stars and Stripes announces that *Doonesbury* has become "too political" and drops it. When the paper receives nearly 300 letters of protest, mainly from young enlisted men and their families, the strip is reinstated.

September 17 **1973**

The *Lincoln Journal* becomes the first paper to move *Doonesbury* from the comic page to the editorial page. In the years that follow, many other papers follow suit.

Often printed as a birth announcement,
"Baby Woman" became a baby tee, size XXXS.

48

—WILLIAM SIMON

49

The prize: 50% off
on large fries.

55

April 20 **1974**

Joanie Caucus is accepted into law school at Boston University after 300 students sign a petition requesting that she be admitted. Joanie also receives acceptances from Georgetown, Golden Gate State, and U.C. Berkeley. She goes to Berkeley.

55

August 2 **1974**

The San Francisco Chronicle drops *Doonesbury* for one day, resulting in 2,000 calls from irate readers. Berkeley law students hold a press conference to announce their intention to picket, and to sue if the strip is dropped permanently.

Boston on the march--and nobody got hit.

MR. PRESIDENT,
MR. PRESIDENT!

1975~1979

"There is no way to defend his art as Art."

—EARL BAKER RUTH
Governor of American Samoa, 1976

Perks: The job came with mansion, limo, drivers, bodyguards, and housegirls.

—HUNTER S. THOMPSON
Writer

WHAT IS IT, MACARTHUR?

EXCELLENCY, THESE TWO WOMEN CRAVE AN AUDIENCE WITH YOU. THERE SEEMS TO BE A DISPUTE OVER A BABY...

OKAY, LADIES— WHAT'S ALL THIS ABOUT?

EXCELLENCY, THIS WOMAN CLAIMS MY BABY HERE IS HERS!

IT IS, EXCELLENCY! EVERYONE KNOWS THIS IS MY CHILD!

HE'S MY BABY, I TELL YOU! HE'S GOT MY BLUE EYES!

DON'T LISTEN TO HER, EXCELLENCY! SHE'S A WELFARE MOTHER AND JUST WANTS ANOTHER DEPENDENT!

YOU KNOW, THIS DISPUTE HAS A RING OF FAMILIARITY TO IT... I BELIEVE THERE'S A BIBLICAL PRECEDENT... AND A SOLUTION!

WHAT IS IT, SIRE?

WAIT A MINUTE... IT'S COMING TO ME... IT'S COMING TO ME...

I'VE GOT IT!— CUT THE KID IN HALF!

HMMM... THAT SOUNDS FAIR..

ARE YOU CRAZY?!

May 5 1975

Trudeau becomes the first comic strip artist to win the Pulitzer Prize for Editorial Cartooning. The Editorial Cartoonists' Society passes a resolution condemning the Pulitzer Prize committee. Trudeau, assured the award was irrevocable, supports the resolution.

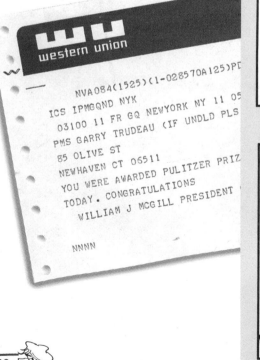

Q .... Why is satire such an effective form of social control?

A .... Because at its rotten little core, it's unfair. It's rude and uncivil. It lacks balance and proportion, and it obeys none of the normal rules of engagement. Satire picks a one-sided fight, and the more its intended target reacts, the more its practitioner gains the advantage. And as if that weren't enough, this savage, unregulated sport is protected by the United States Constitution. Cool, huh?

June 12 **1975**

An exhibition of Trudeau cartoons opens in Washington, D.C., for the benefit of the National Women's Political Caucus. Reports *The Washington Post*, "Almost 1,000 people tried to get into the small gallery. Observed one disgruntled man, "If these women can't run an art show, how do they expect to run the country?" Sniffs the *Post's* critic, "There is no way to defend his art as Art."

February 10 1976

Andy Lippincott, a gay, is introduced in *Doonesbury*, causing dozens of newspapers to drop the sequence. Some papers offer to mail copies of the offending strips to readers.

Trudeau travels with the press corps covering Gerald Ford's visit to China, and becomes the first American cartoonist to toss a Frisbee on the Great Wall.

The Ugly American Frisbee All-Stars also included the President's daughter, Susan.

Millions of Mao buttons, inescapable in 1975, were to become overnight collector's items.

His Excellency takes the air with love-slave food-taster Honey Huan.

TELL ME, HONEY—SINCE YOU'RE THE ONLY TRANSLATOR IN CHINA WHO CAN STILL UNDERSTAND THE CHAIRMAN, HOW FAITHFULLY DO YOU ACTUALLY CARRY OUT HIS WISHES?

WELL, SIR, HE CHANGES HIS MIND A LOT, AND ALTHOUGH HIS WORD IS ABSOLUTE LAW, I HAVE TO ACCOUNT FOR THAT.

FOR INSTANCE, LAST MONDAY, HE TOLD ME TO HAVE THE GREAT WALL TORN DOWN, SINCE IT'S A SYMBOL OF ANCIENT TYRANNY. ON TUESDAY, I REPORTED THAT ALL 1,500 MILES HAD BEEN DISMANTLED.

THEN ON THURSDAY, HE TOLD ME HE HAD HAD SECOND THOUGHTS, AND THAT HE WANTED THE WALL REBUILT AT ONCE.

FRIDAY NIGHT, I TOLD HIM THAT I HAD PERSONALLY DIRECTED THE MOBILIZATION OF 20 MILLION WORKERS, AND THAT THE ENTIRE WALL HAD BEEN RESTORED TO ITS FORMER CONDITION.

ACTUALLY, I SPENT THE WHOLE WEEK WATCHING T.V., BUT HE THINKS I'M A GENIUS.

IN A WAY, YOU ARE, HONEY..

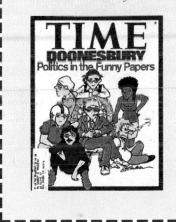

Raved one critic about Thudpucker's single for the Slade campaign: "Sure, it might appear putrid (the B-side is 'Ginny's Song—Disco Version'), but it is appealing enough."

Seven newspapers drop a strip that has Uncle Duke calling President Ford's son a "pot head."

"'There are moments when the press is unfair to anyone who's a public figure,' Ford said, referring to his portrayal as a 'pot head' yesterday in *Doonesbury*. 'But they must make their own moral judgment on that.'"

—*Washington Star, January 20, 1977*

March 22 **1976**

Trudeau is selected as the tenth most admired world figure by high school seniors in a nationwide poll, placing him below Alexander Solzhenitsyn and Ralph Nader, but just ahead of Ronald Reagan and Pope Paul.

Over 30 newspapers drop the strip showing Joanie and Rick in bed together (at the time, neither was married). The editor of *The Huntington Herald-Dispatch* informs his readers, "When I first saw it, I thought it was two guys in bed." *The Bangor Daily News* blocks out the last frame, replacing it with the weather forecast ("Fair, cold, highs in the 30s"). A group of M.I.T. students pickets *The Boston Globe* with signs reading, "Joanie, we forgive you."

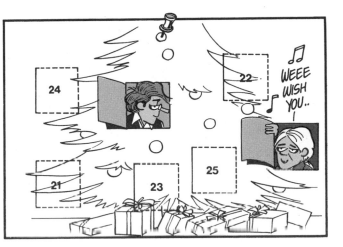

Q .... Your family worried, didn't they?

A .... Pretty much incessantly. The accolades, when they happened, came more as a source of relief than pride. My grandmother in particular thought no good could possibly come of cartooning. Every summer when I was growing up she would plead with my parents to send me to Outward Bound, because she had read in *Life* that the counselors were very good at reaching troubled teens.

Q .... Did they make you go?

A .... No. In those days, Outward Bound was stocked with the soft sons of the well-off, who, in the absence of war, couldn't think of any other way to build character in their progeny. So they sent them off for three weeks of kayaking and rappelling and subsisting on roots and earthworms, and let's face it, I would have perished. I think my parents knew that.

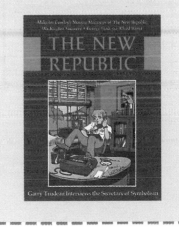

JOANIE GRADUATES

"She never showed up for classes, but she was one of Boalt Hall's most famous and beloved students. Yesterday, Joanie Caucus (B.A., Colorado College, 1956) received her juris doctor degree from the UC law school where her mentor — cartoonist Garry Trudeau — had placed her application three years ago. Trudeau, creator of the comic strip *Doonesbury*, was guest speaker at the exercises. Caucus, shown above as a mortarboard on an empty seat, reportedly received a job offer from an actual southern California law firm. She had no comment."

— *San Francisco Examiner,*
May 22, 1977

Eighteen years later, Joanie continues to receive alumni mailings, at taxpayers' expense.

Following Duke's tour of duty, Trudeau was commissioned to paint a portrait of him to hang in the U. S. Embassy.

A Doonesbury Special, an animated film, debuts on NBC. It is later nominated for an Academy Award and wins the Special Jury Prize at the Cannes Film Festival

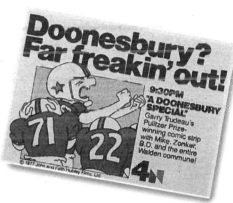

Wrote TV critic Marvin Kittman: *"I found it interesting to watch those Walden commune weirdos."*

December 11 1977

The Exxon Educational Foundation announces a $100,000 Joanie Caucus Exxon Fellowship Program to aid women over 30 who want to become lawyers.

February 9 **1978**

In its review of Jimmy
Thudpucker's Greatest Hits,
the *Buffalo Courier Express*
noted, "Thudpucker, who
was once part of the
solution, is now part of
the problem."

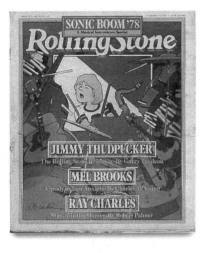

*A legend's legend: Jimmy's second
Rolling Stone cover.*

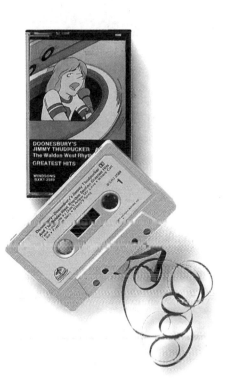

WIIN radio host Wizard Wayne boasts to the New York Daily News: *"I've known Jimmy Thudpucker most of his life. I used to date his sister Serena."*

June 16 **1978**

Doonesbury urges readers to find out more about "Koreagate" by sending in a newspaper coupon to Speaker of the House Tip O'Neill, who is not pleased when over a dozen sacks of mail arrive. Prior to the strip's release, an O'Neill aide had called Universal Press Syndicate and attempted to stop its publication.

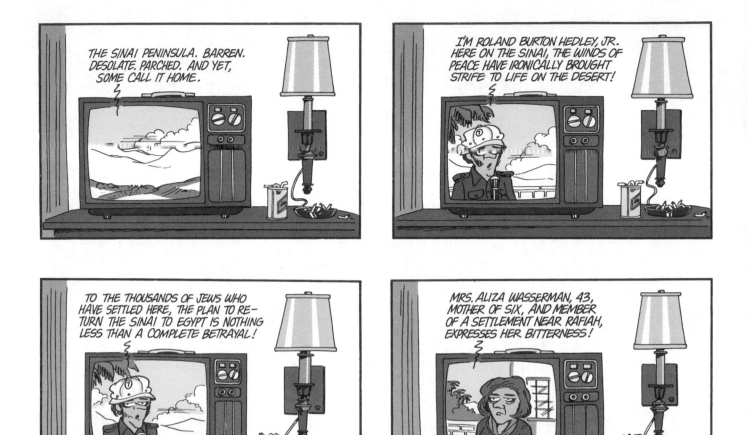

Q · · · · What's the deal with Zonker's beach in Malibu?

A · · · · Well, it's not really a beach. It's a beach accessway. In the late 70s, the California Coastal Commission liberated a number of public beaches that had been, in effect, privatized by residents who owned property in front of them. Naturally, the new access routes were not popular with folks accustomed to thinking of the beaches as their own, and the redwood sign marking the Zonker Harris Memorial Accessway was vandalized within 24 hours.

The Republican caucus of the Virginia General Assembly censures Trudeau for his satirical treatment of Senator John Warner and his wife Elizabeth Taylor. The 28 Republicans vote unanimously to express their "outrage and indignation." Fumed the motion's sponsor, State Senator Wiley Mitchell, "I don't think we should sit placidly by and let the gnomes of the world run over us without expressing indignation."

May 28 **1979**

When the *Washington Post* suspends *Doonesbury*, the strip is read on talk shows and TV news programs, and even appears in the White House News Summary "as a service to our readers." Jody Powell tells a White House press briefing that he might ask the Justice Department to look into the strip's disappearance.

— MARION BARRY, JR.

Mistaking Zeke for a raccoon

Awarded to G. B. Trudeau, age 12, for achievement in the prone position.

.. AND NOW.. SOME MORE MELLOW SOUNDS.. FOR YOUR NATURAL LIFESTYLE...

A crate of original *Doonesbury* drawings is stolen from the office of Trudeau's answering service, only to be recovered in a police raid on the Sunshine Girls Escort Service in Hamden, Connecticut. Sunshine's unlucky social director is subsequently convicted of first-degree larceny, largely on the strength of Trudeau's ability to recognize his own work in court.

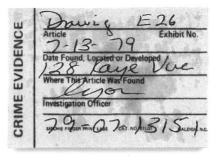

The perpetrator was nabbed at the Canadian border.

CLASS OF 1979. I GREET YOU ON THE OCCASION OF MY TENTH COMMENCEMENT ADDRESS TO THE GRADUATING CLASS OF THIS UNIVERSITY..

I NEED NOT TELL YOU IT HAS BEEN A REMARKABLE DECADE. AND AS THE LAST CLASS TO GRADUATE IN THE SEVENTIES, IT IS FITTING THAT YOU ARE NO LESS REMARKABLE.

AS YOU KNOW, A RECORD NUMBER OF YOU HAVE BEEN ACCEPTED AT TOP LAW AND MEDICAL SCHOOLS. MANY OTHERS HAVE RECEIVED PRESTIGIOUS AWARDS AND FELLOWSHIPS FOR STUDY ABROAD.

AM I PROUD OF YOU? DO I TAKE MORE THAN ORDINARY PLEASURE IN THIS ASTONISHING RECORD?

BY WAY OF ANSWER, I WOULD LIKE TO SHARE WITH YOU THE OPENING WORDS OF MY GRADUATION SPEECH TO THE CLASS OF 1970..

"ATTENTION: WILL THE STUDENTS WHO TRASHED MY OFFICE LAST NIGHT PLEASE RETURN THE DIPLOMAS?"

West Coast papers drop a sequence linking Governor Jerry Brown to alleged underworld figure Sidney Korshak. In a nice touch, the only papers outside of California to kill the strip are located in Reno and Las Vegas.

BUILD WE MUST!

BOY, I HAD A **CORKER** OF A DREAM LAST NIGHT, GANG!

HERE WE GO AGAIN..

WHAT WAS IT ABOUT, ELLIE?

WELL, IT WAS PART OF A CONTINUING SERIES ABOUT SISTERHOOD..

IN IT, I DREAMT THAT THE EQUAL RIGHTS AMENDMENT WAS PASSED UNANIMOUSLY BY ALL FIFTY STATES!

YOU WERE DREAMING, ALL RIGHT.

ANYTHING ELSE?

YEAH. JUST BEFORE I WOKE UP, THERE WAS FULL COMPLIANCE ACROSS THE LAND!

WOW.. YOU SURE HAVE INTERESTING DREAMS, ELLIE.

THANKS, LILLY. WHAT DO YOU DREAM ABOUT, HOWARD?

MY NEXT TWINKIE.

HEY, ME, TOO! DO YOU SUCK THE CREAMY PART OUT FIRST?

GBTrudeau

1980~1984

"Anybody who can draw bad pictures of the White House four times in a row and succeed knows something I don't."

—AL CAPP, CREATOR OF L'IL ABNER

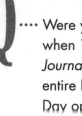

Q .... Were you shocked when *The Wall Street Journal* turned over its entire New Year's Day op-ed page to reprinting your *fin-de-decade* strips?

A .... Well, there was a little soul-searching, but the fact was, taken as a whole, the series did reveal a markedly conservative perspective on a wide variety of social issues. And that was before I had children. My guess is that the *Journal* reprinted it as a welcome turn of events, although it's also possible they had nothing else to run that day.

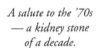

A salute to the '70s — a kidney stone of a decade.

February 11 **1980**

The presidential candidacy of Republican Congressman John Anderson receives an unexpected boost through the attentions of Mike Doonesbury. At first Anderson calls the coverage "nifty," but later in the campaign, after Barbara Bush dubs him "the *Doonesbury* candidate," Anderson has second thoughts.

Confided the candidate's wife, Keke, to Playboy, *"With Garry Trudeau, you had the most respected advance man in politics."*

— JOHN ANDERSON

I PROPOSE WE QUIETLY DISBAND AT HALF-TIME.

Q ···· Given its volatile nature, the hostage crisis in Iran must have been a difficult subject for cartoonists.

A ···· It was. Early on, I had to recall and retool material. Oddly enough — considering how much I was writing about the crisis — *Doonesbury* was one of the few things the Iranian students failed to censor from the hostages' reading material. They had made a familiar assumption — that nothing of consequence could be found in a comic strip.

— WILLIAM F. KEOGH, JR.
on the strips he received while in captivity

"Gotta run — my government's collapsing."

October 25 **1980**

More than two dozen newspapers drop "The Mysterious World of Reagan's Brain," a week-long sequence that runs on the eve of the 1980 election. One of those papers, *The Indianapolis Star,* receives 850 calls of protest before it agrees to reinstate the strip. Opines the Rochester *Times-Union,* "Any voters who might be influenced by something they read on the comic page probably shouldn't be voting."

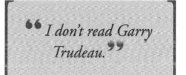

SO AS GRAND HOOTER OF THE EXALTED ORDER OF COLORADO SPRINGS CARIBOU, I GIVE YOU A GENUINE HERO, THE 53RD HOSTAGE, AMBASSADOR *DUKE!*

COLORADO SPRINGS CARIBOU LODGE

HOOT! HOOT! HOOT! HOOT!

THANK YOU. THANK YOU VERY MUCH FOR THAT WEIRD WELCOME. I'M VERY TOUCHED.

COLORADO SPRINGS CARIBOU LODGE

HOWEVER, SINCE YOUR HONORARIUM BARELY COVERS EXPENSES, I'M AFRAID I'M GOING TO HAVE TO PASS ON THE SPEECH AND JUST TAKE YOUR QUESTIONS INSTEAD.

COLORADO SPRINGS CARIBOU LODGE

MR. DUKE, WERE YOU SUBJECTED TO ANY PHYSICAL TORTURE WHILE YOU WERE A HOSTAGE?

AS A MATTER OF FACT, I WAS. DURING MY FIRST WEEK OF CAPTIVITY, I WAS GAGGED AND MANACLED TO THE SPRAY NOZZLE IN A HOTEL SHOWER STALL.

COLORADO SPRINGS CARIBOU LODGE

WHILE THE GUARDS CHANTED THE KORAN IN THE BACKGROUND, ONE OF THE FEMALE STUDENTS POURED HONEY AND FEATHERS ALL OVER THE TOP OF MY HEAD. LAUGHING SADISTICALLY, SHE THEN REACHED FOR THE TOP BUTTON OF HER SHIRT, AND.. AND..

COLORADO SPRINGS CARIBOU LODGE

AND *WHAT?* AND *WHAT?*

I'M SORRY, IT'S.. IT'S TOO PAINFUL TO RECALL FOR ONLY 500 BUCKS.

COLORADO SPRINGS CARIBOU LODGE

January 24 **1981**

Last seen before an Iranian firing squad on September 7, 1979, Uncle Duke is released, after the other 52 American hostages, from captivity. Cheers the Lexington, Ky. *Herald*, "Welcome home, well done — whatever it was you did over there."

Reported UPI, "Uncle Duke is alive and well and probably stoned somewhere in Wiesbaden, Germany."

The Detroit Free Press announces the Zonker Harris Testimonial Tan Off. Cash prizes total $210.

He came to tan: Zonker takes his event at the 1981 Gerald R. Ford Pro-am Summer Biathlon.

HMM.. MAYBE THERE **IS** SOMETHING TO THIS BORN-AGAIN STUFF..

ERRATA:
THE WEDDING IS ON THURSDAY, JUNE 18. THE NAME OF THE BRIDEGOON IS "RICK," NOT "BICK".

Thanks

— James G. Watt

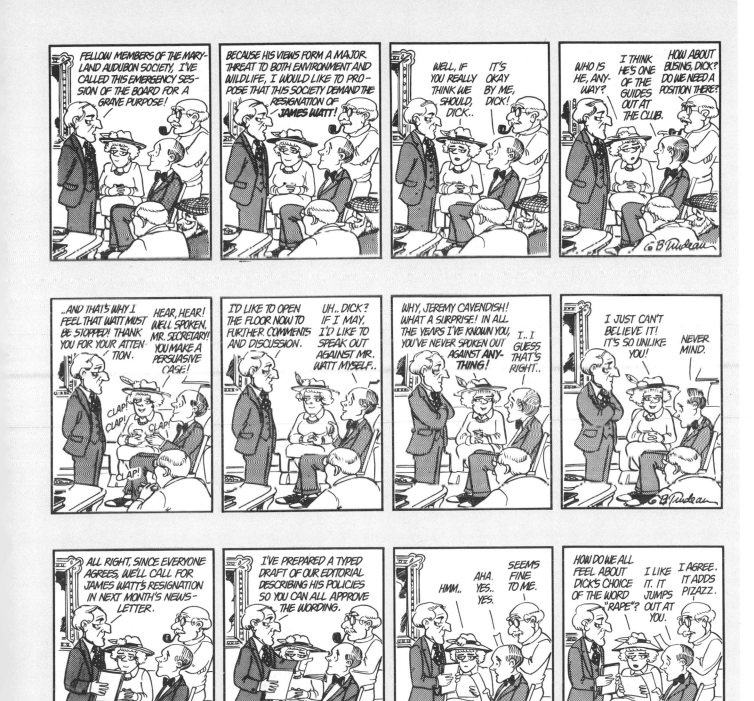

Neither did little boys.

In the heartland, a heart to heart.

February 7 **1982**

In response to a suicide threat by EPA staffer and *Doonesbury* character Ted Simpson, the agency issues an internal memo outlining new "security measures" for windows and ledges.

> **"** *The pictorial narrative, or comic strip, like every other dioptric art, contains at least two messages, one denoted and the other connoted. But when we contemplate the plants as the plants talk to Zonker, are we aware of a true system of signs in an analogical representation, or are we stuck with a simple agglutination of symbols?* **"**

— JOHN LEONARD
reviewing a Doonesbury *book in* The New York Times

November 8 **1982**

Trudeau announces a 20-month leave of absence, claiming that "investigative cartooning is a young man's game." Farewell editorials appear across the country. Laments former President Jimmy Carter, "I'm heartbroken."

November 9 1982

Zonker Harris receives one vote for the governorship in Illinois.

*After twelve years,
the Class of '83 moves on.*

An American runner, jogging through Moscow wearing a Zonker T-shirt, is stopped several times by Russians who ask if the T-shirt likeness is a caricature of Trotsky. They said with evident political concern, "You know, Trotsky is not accepted over here." A few, with a different perception, asked, "Is that really Lenin on the American T-shirt?"

January 2 1983

Doonesbury ceases publication. The Wisconsin State Assembly issues a declaration pleading for "public calm in the face of this grave crisis."

ACTION!

HI, ED, WHAT'S UP?

"FAREWELL TO ALMS"
1983 SCENE / 1 TAKE

RECORD UNEMPLOYMENT, STAGGERING DEFICITS, AND THE RENEWAL OF AN INSANE ARMS RACE, SIR.

GREAT! STAY THE COURSE!

CUT! OKAY, THAT'S A WRAP! STRIKE THE SET!

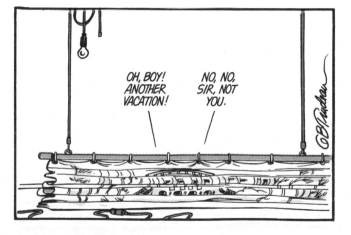

OH, BOY! ANOTHER VACATION!

NO, NO, SIR, NOT YOU.

PLAYBILL

WILBUR THEATRE

Doonesbury

"Doonesbury, A Musical" opened at Broadway's Biltmore Theater on November 21, 1983, earning Grammy and Drama Desk Award nominations.

171

September 1984

Doonesbury returns to syndication. The Wisconsin Assembly repeals its 20-month state of emergency.

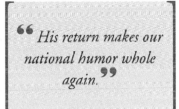

> **"** *His return makes our national humor whole again.* **"**

—SENATOR EDWARD KENNEDY

Q ···· You got hammered a lot for your Reagan strips during the 1984 election. Were you surprised?

A ···· Yes, but I shouldn't have been. By that time, Reagan was so universally regarded as "nice" that even the mildest criticism of him was judged churlish and mean-spirited. Obviously Reagan's unique blend of manly jingoism and sunny cluelessness had been a tonic for a nation yearning to feel good about itself again. But his presidency always reminded me of a remark made by a woman to Heywood Broun following Secretariat's victory in the Triple Crown. After the trauma of Vietnam and Watergate, she said, Secretariat had "restored her faith in humanity." I like to think Reagan was the Secretariat of the eighties.

Escondido Times-Advocate editor Will Corbin drops *Doonesbury*, writing, "If it's the only basis upon which a decision to buy this newspaper is made, then I might as well be selling shoes."

Escondido Times-Advocate editor Will Corbin selling shoes.

177

1985~1989

"I read *Doonesbury* every day. What else do you want to know?"

—SAL CONSIGLIO, OWNER OF SALLY'S PIZZA, OFTEN MENTIONED IN THE STRIP

Admonished Quincy Jones, "Check your egos at the door."

Public criticism of Senator Jake Garn's "ultimate junket" aboard the space shuttle is led by *Doonesbury*, which dubs him "Barfin' Jake" (later shortened to "B.J." by his fellow astronauts).

Among Garn's chores in space: playing with 10 children's toys.

June 3 1985

Trudeau's syndicate convinces him to withdraw "Silent Scream: The Prequel," a week of strips satirizing an anti-abortion film. *The New Republic* magazine runs all six cartoons in its June 10 issue.

Panel 1: AS THE MOMENT APPROACHES, TIMMY SEEMS ALMOST OBLIVIOUS TO THE CHARGED DEBATE THAT ATTENDS HIS FATE.

Panel 2: MINUTES LATER, THE DIE IS CAST. THE MOTHER HAS MADE THE UNCONSCIONABLE DECISION THAT SETS IN MOTION THE DOCTOR'S GRISLY PROCEDURE.

Panel 3: THE FINAL SECONDS. BY STUDYING HIS MOUTH THROUGH STOP-ACTION IMAGING, WE CAN DETERMINE TIMMY'S FINAL WORDS, WHICH ARE, ALMOST CERTAINLY, "REPEAL ROE V. WADE."

Panel 4: COMING UP: TIMMY REMEMBERED.

Panel 5: "HIS LOVE OF COUNTRY, HIS GENEROSITY FOR THOSE LESS FORTUNATE, HIS DISTINCTIVE ART..

Panel 6: ..AND HIS WINNING AND COMPASSIONATE PERSONA MAKE HIM ONE OF OUR MOST REMARKABLE AND DISTINGUISHED AMERICANS..

Panel 7: ..AND ONE WHO TRULY DID IT HIS WAY."
— Ronald Reagan
May 23, 1985

Panel 8 (photo caption): MEDAL OF FREEDOM RECIPIENT FRANK SINATRA DOING IT HIS WAY WITH TOMMY "FATSO" MARSON, DON CARLO GAMBINO, RICHARD "NERVES" FUSCO, JIMMY "THE WEASEL" FRATIANNO, JOSEPH GAMBINO AND GREG DEPALMA.

Panel 9: "HE HAS CARRIED ON HIS CRAFT WITH DISTINCTION AND HIGH PROFESSIONALISM..

Panel 10: HE HAS APPLIED HIS TALENTS TO THE BENEFIT OF MANKIND..

Panel 11: ..AND TO THE UPLIFTING OF THE HUMAN SPIRIT."
— Citation for honorary degree, Stevens Institute, May 23, 1985

Panel 12 (photo caption): DR. FRANCIS SINATRA UPLIFTING THE SPIRITS OF ALLEGED HUMAN ANIELLO DELLACROCE, LATER CHARGED WITH THE MURDER OF GAMBINO FAMILY MEMBER CHARLEY CALISE.

June 13 1985

Numerous newspapers drop a series critical of Reagan's presentation of the Medal of Freedom to Frank Sinatra. The following week, Trudeau is denounced by a New Jersey congressman on the floor of the U.S. House of Representatives.

> " He's as funny as a tumor. "

— FRANK SINATRA
from the stage at Carnegie Hall

Q .... Did Sinatra ever sue?

A .... No, but his lawyer weighed in. He sent my employers a letter saying that I had completely misrepresented Mr. Sinatra's actions on such and such a day. Our position was that of *course* my portrayal of the incident was inaccurate—I'd made it up. We never heard from him again.

October 1 **1985**

A Florida State legislator introduces the so-called "*Doonesbury* Bill," which challenges a Palm Beach law requiring servants to carry ID cards. The president of the Florida Senate notes, "What I know about the ordinance is what I read in *Doonesbury*." The bill passes nine months later.

"*Freedom's freedom,*" *said the bill's sponsor,*
"*You can't put a card-carrying thing in it.*
Let the commies do that."

November 28 **1985**

Trudeau, Charles Schulz, and Milt Caniff organize 175 syndicated cartoonists to focus attention on world hunger by devoting their Thanksgiving Day strips to the subject.

> *"Naw, I thought they were funny. They were cute."*

—CLINT EASTWOOD
commenting on Doonesbury *strips*

"Say it ain't so, Trudeau!" pleads the headline of a Wisconsin paper. Uncle Duke, discovered one morning "looking more inert than usual," is pronounced dead. *The St. Petersburg Times* runs a full obituary, as the *Paterson (N.J.) News* laments, "Duke was the kind of swine you couldn't help but like." The bizarre tragedy is ultimately softened by the revelation that Duke was not dead, but merely zombified and sold into slavery.

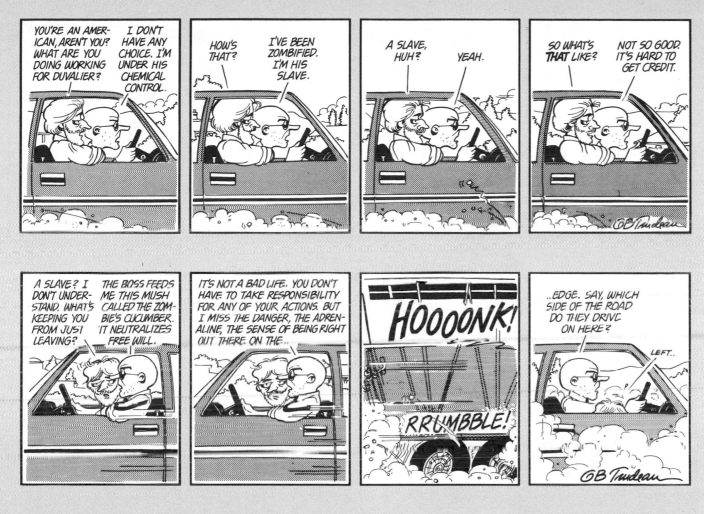

April 14 **1986**

Mark Slackmeyer broadcasts "Sleaze on Parade," the definitive list of Reaganite "back-scratchers, till-dippers, and conscience-cutters." Numerous papers drop the strip, among them *The Los Angeles Times.*

May 9 **1986**

The "Save the Gown" campaign urges readers to help "stabilize" Nancy Reagan's sagging inaugural gown. The Smithsonian sets up a special phone number to handle contributions and responses. Writes one Beverly Hills businessman, "Do something before it's too late."

202

Doonesbury tour of "Contra Country" tracks the freedom fighters in Miami. Miffed Contra leader Arturo Cruz calls it "amusing satire," but says he prefers *Hagar the Horrible.*

Doonesbury satirizes a Reagan speech by pinpointing Harlingen, Texas, as the likely target for a Sandinistan invasion. Sheriff Alex Perez requests riot gear, vowing, "If we don't get it, I guess we'll have to fight with tree limbs." The Harlingen Chamber of Commerce votes to spend $22,898 for a tourism ad campaign based on strips about the town.

January 5 1987

Readers "clip 'n' save" pieces of "the Iranscam puzzle," hoping Trudeau will complete it. He doesn't. Numerous frustrated readers write in for "the missing piece." One woman speculates: "I think my cat ate it."

Boopsie channels "Hunk-Ra" and joins the "totally historic" California Self-Esteem Task Force, an entity many mistakenly assume Trudeau invented. Says Task Force creator John Vasconcellos, "Satire is the highest form of indirect compliment."

"We thought the *Doonesbury* gang was pulling our leg again. We stand chastened and humbled to confess that we could not imagine anything with such a horse's-fanny title could be anything but make-believe."

— *Editorial, Salem Statesman-Journal*

Mike Doonesbury is assigned to write condom ads for television. Papers in Montana, Utah, and Texas pull the series.

Post-modern protection, to go.

EMPLOYEE-OF-THE-MONTH SAL DOONESBURY TALKS ABOUT "DR. WHOOPEE"...

THE JOB ISN'T REALLY ABOUT MARKET SHARE — IT'S ABOUT PEOPLE, AND SOLVING THEIR PROBLEMS..

LAST MONTH I GOT AN URGENT CALL FROM A LARGE SORORITY AT A WELL-KNOWN EASTERN COLLEGE. SPRING BREAK WAS 12 HOURS AWAY, AND THEY NEEDED PROTECTION.

"I QUICKLY ROUTED THE ORDER ONTO OUR PRIORITY SATELLITE LINE, INSTANTLY ALERTING THE HOME OFFICE IN FLAGSTAFF..."

"WITHIN MINUTES, THE ORDER WAS PROCESSED AND PACKED AND WINGING ITS WAY TO THE ANXIOUS SORORITY SISTERS..."

'EVENING, MISS!

DOCTOR WHOOPEE! YOU MADE IT!

"DR. WHOOPEE," WHERE **PEOPLE** ARE JOB ONE.

SERVICE WITH A SMILE, **NOT** A SMIRK!

"Until further notice, the *Log Cabin Democrat* has pulled the *Doonesbury* comic strip because of its mature subject matter. Readers who wish to view the strip may come by the *Log Cabin* office, 1058 Front St., during business hours, which are 7:30 a.m. to 5:30 p.m., Monday through Friday."

— *Editorial Note*
Log Cabin Democrat,
February 23, 1987

213

March 1987

Roland Hedley embarks upon a "Return to Reagan's Brain" to jar 10000 Irancram memories. Once again, some editors pull the series.

215

Callers jam White House switchboards after Ron Headrest provides readers with the number to call for "rock-solid information on safe sex." Later in the day the White House takes revenge: White House spokesman Marlin Fitzwater orders the callers be given the number of Trudeau's employer.

Said a puzzled Fitzwater, "I wonder why he did that? Mischief, I guess."

217

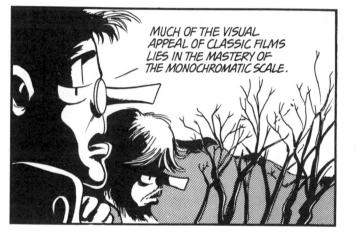

December 3 **1987**

Defending Larry Flynt's satire of Jerry Falwell before the Supreme Court, attorney Alan Isaacman argues that the parody is entitled to the same First Amendment protection as *Doonesbury* spoofs of George Bush.

The Prince of Inner Space.

225

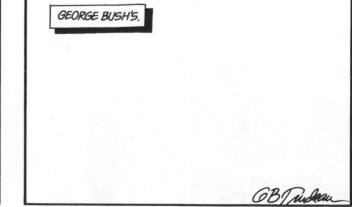

Q .... Was the Bush stuff personal?

A .... Of course not. It's never personal. At the risk of sounding like Sonny Corleone, it's my job. The Bushes never got that. Jeb Bush once drew me aside at the Republican Convention and said he had only two words for me: "Walk softly." Now, telling a cartoonist to walk softly is like asking a professional wrestler to show a little class. It's just not a productive suggestion. I went home and redoubled my efforts.

MR. BUSH, IF I UNDERSTAND YOUR POSITION CORRECTLY, YOU BELIEVE THAT ABORTION IS MURDER ...

EXCEPT IN SPECIAL CASES, YES.

YOU ALSO ENDORSE THE DEATH PENALTY FOR MURDERERS...

SURE, BUT...

DOES THIS MEAN YOU FAVOR EXECUTING THE MILLIONS OF WOMEN WHO CHOOSE TO HAVE ABORTIONS?

NO, NO, I NOW SEE THAT THESE WOMEN ARE VIC-TIMS WHO NEED HELP AND LOVE.

THE CRIMINAL AS VICTIM? SIR, ISN'T THAT BEING SQUISHY-SOFT ON CRIME?

UH...OKAY, THEN, WE'LL HOLD THEIR *DOCTORS* ACCOUNTABLE!

THEN YOU FAVOR EXECUTING THOUSANDS OF DOCTORS?

LOOK, WE'LL EXECUTE SOMEBODY, OKAY? I'M STILL SORTING OUT THE DETAILS!

HOW ABOUT EXECUTING THE DOCTORS' LAWYERS?

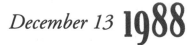

December 13 1988

The *Winston-Salem Journal* drops a strip on the R.J. Reynolds Tobacco Co. because "it would be personally offensive to its employees." It is the first time the strip has been pulled in deference to a corporation.

Panel 1: I CAN'T BELIEVE WE JUST LEFT LITTLE NO-NAME WITH ZONKER. / SHE'LL BE FINE.

Panel 2: WHAT IF HE JUST PLOPS HER IN FRONT OF THE TUBE AND ZONES OUT ALL DAY?

Panel 3: HE WON'T. HE TOLD ME HIMSELF HE DOESN'T BELIEVE IN UNSUPERVISED TELEVISION.

Panel 4: OKAY, NOW, THAT'S CALLED "CROSS-DRESSING." CAN YOU SAY "CROSS-DRESSING"? / TRY THE PEARLS, PHIL!

Panel 5: ZONKER? / MIKE!

Panel 6: HOW'D IT GO? / BETTER GET IN HERE! QUICK!

Panel 7: WHAT? THE BABY...? / THANK GOD YOU'RE HERE!

Panel 8: WHAT? WHAT'S *WRONG*? / UH... NOTHING. IT'S FIVE. I'M OFF DUTY.

Panel 9: NIGHTY, NIGHT, PUMPKIN! / OH, I ALMOST FORGOT TO TELL YOU...

Panel 10: TODAY SHE CALLED ME "MAMA"! ISN'T THAT *WILD*? SHE CALLED THE BABY-SITTER "MAMA"!

Panel 11: (no dialogue)

Panel 12: ALWAYS A MOMENT EVERY MOTHER TREASURES, ZONK. / WELL, I THOUGHT SO, SO I VIDEO-TAPED IT.

I'M BAD! I'M BAAD...

237

Panel 1:
ROOTS.
GET **OUT** THERE, CHRISTIAN SCUM! THE LIONS ARE **HUNGRY!**

Panel 2:
A SPLENDID ENTERTAINMENT, EH, FLAVIUS IMPERVIOUS?
PERHAPS. BUT IT PANDERS TO SUCH BASE, MOB INSTINCTS.

Panel 3:
DON'T BE SO CONDESCENDING, FLAVIUS! THIS IS WHAT THE ROMAN PUBLIC WANTS! NO ONE IS FORCING THEM TO BE HERE!
SURE, BUT...

Panel 4:
HAVE A PITY, MAN! THE EMPIRE IS CRUMBLING AROUND US! IF WATCHING A FEW MARTYRS GET TORN APART HELPS PEOPLE GET THEIR MINDS OFF THEIR PROBLEMS, THEN I'M **PROUD** TO BE PART OF IT!

Panel 5:
BY JUPITER, YOU'RE RIGHT. I NEVER THOUGHT OF IT THAT WAY. BY OFFERING A PUBLIC DISTRACTION, YOU'RE SOFTENING THE ROUGH EDGES OF LIFE!

Panel 6:
YOU'RE A GOOD MAN, GERALDO RIVERIBUS.
I TRY.

©B. Trudeau

A three-week series in which Congresswoman Lacey Davenport dis covers that her aide Andy Lippincott is suffering from AIDS is widely discussed. A few papers drop the series, but many AIDS activists approve. Christian Heran, an AIDS sufferer in San Francisco, tells UPI, "The epidemic does have its funny side."

August 13 **1989**

700 people clip Mr. Butts'
coupon promising free
cigarettes ("recipient must
be under-aged") and mail
it to the Tobacco Institute.
When asked what the
response indicated, Institute
spokeswoman Brennan
Dawson notes, "I think
it shows the kids read
the comics."

*Buttsie and Mr. Jay:
The gateway drugs kibitz in Mike's
compromised imagination.*

WE'VE GOT A SPECIAL TREAT ON TAP FOR YOU, NIGHT OWLS! WITH ME RIGHT NOW IS VICE PRESIDENT **DAN QUAYLE**, WHO WAS RECENTLY NAMED "1989 FATHER OF THE YEAR" BY THE NATIONAL FATHER'S DAY COMMITTEE!

"1989 FATHER OF THE YEAR"! THAT'S QUITE AN HONOR, MR. VICE PRESIDENT!

YES, IT IS, MARK...

BUT, YOU KNOW, BASICALLY IT'S A TRIBUTE TO **MY** FATHER! HE'S THE ONE WHO SET THE EXAMPLE FOR ME IN THE PARENTING DEPARTMENT!

FOR INSTANCE, ONCE A WEEK, HE'D MAKE ME SIT DOWN AND RECITE **GOLDEN'S RULE**, WHICH GOES "DO WITH OTHERS WHAT THEY WOULD HAVE YOU UNDO..."

"...OR WHAT THEY THEMSELVES DO TO TRESPASS AGAINST THOSE WHO DO IT WHETHER OR NOT THEY...THEY...UM...

WHATEVER. THE IMPORTANT THING WAS THAT YOU GUYS TALKED!

THAT'S RIGHT, MARK! WHICH IS WHY THE CHIP DIDN'T FALL VERY FAR FROM THE BLOCK!

Q .... Any repercussions from the Teheran Critics Circle strips?

A .... Only a temporary security upgrade. That spring I attended the American Booksellers Association Convention, and the organizers insisted that any author who had taken a public position on the *fatwa* be accompanied by a bodyguard. I spent two days strolling around the booths, trying to make small talk with booksellers while my intense companion scrutinized the crowds for potential assassins.

The worst part of having a bodyguard is that you get used to it. When he finally put me in a car for the airport, I don't believe I ever felt more vulnerable in my life.

HI! RECOVERED PROBLEM TANNIST ZONKER HARRIS HERE!

IF YOU'RE LIKE ME, BY NOW YOU'VE KICKED YOUR DANGEROUS SUN HABIT. SO HOW DO YOU CONTINUE LEADING AN ACTIVE, OUTDOOR LIFE WITHOUT RUNNING THE RISK OF ACQUIRING AN UNSIGHTLY TAN?

EASY, NOW THAT THERE'S NERD-CARE™! NERD-CARE™ IS THE MEDICALLY PROVEN BLEACHING LOTION THAT 3 OUT OF 4 PROFESSIONAL COMPUTER PROGRAMMERS SAY THEY WOULD WANT WITH THEM IF THEY WERE STRANDED ON A DESERT ISLAND.

POP!

TAP! TAP! TAP!

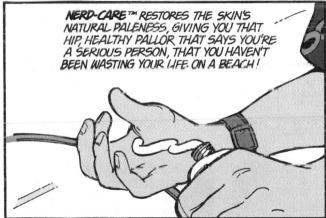

NERD-CARE™ RESTORES THE SKIN'S NATURAL PALENESS, GIVING YOU THAT HIP, HEALTHY PALLOR THAT SAYS YOU'RE A SERIOUS PERSON, THAT YOU HAVEN'T BEEN WASTING YOUR LIFE ON A BEACH!

SO GO AHEAD, LIGHTEN UP WITH NERD-CARE™ FOR THE FINEST IN PALE.

NERD-CARE™
15
paleness factor

NOW AVAILABLE IN PALE, WHITER SHADE OF PALE, AND NEW, MINTY GREEN!

NEW!
NERD-CARE™
15
paleness factor

September 11 **1989**

Doonesbury sequence breaks true story of Barbara Bush's encounter with a rat in the White House swimming pool.

1990~1995

"Vile and disgraceful attack!
Untruthful and scurrilous!"

—Rep. Dick Schulze on Doonesbury, speaking
from the floor of the U.S. House of Representatives

Several papers drop *Doonesbury* series on Dan Quayle's purchase of an anatomically correct gag doll during an official visit to Chile. The Pine Bluff, Arkansas *Commercial* explained, "Those of us in the newspaper business are obliged to cover the tasteless, but we see no reason to publish material on this page that is both tasteless and boring."

Handcrafted in Chile: The anatomically explicit Dan Quayle doll.

Sunday strip features "protest stamps," which Zonker urges readers to affix to correspondence in opposition to proposed postal rate increase. United States Postal Service officials issue an internal alert bulletin. Postmaster General Anthony M. Frank calls the strip "a mistake."

"They're definitely illegal," said a spokesman. The fine: $300.

May 24 1990

Andy Lippincott finally succumbs to AIDS. *The San Francisco Chronicle* runs news of his death on its obituary page, and Andy is remembered by a square in NAMES Project AIDS Memorial Quilt.

Andy's square: Its author takes a few liberties.

October 15 **1990**

In a 20th anniversary profile, Trudeau describes himself as "Joan of Arc's spouse."

Sunshine warriors: Trudeau smuggled in his proxies.

*Full Metal
Buttons:
Commemorating
the Build-up,
1990.*

Q .... You wrote about the Gulf War for almost 250 consecutive days. Overkill?

A .... Possibly, but I was getting great feedback — and ideas — from military personnel in the field. When I finally got over there, the troops invited me aboard their Blackhawks and Bradleys and within a week had me driving a M-1A tank. They were too young — and I was too flushed — to remember Dukakis.

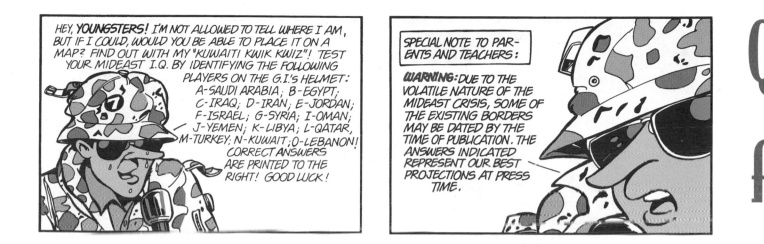

Q .... What an odd way to experience the war.

A .... Well, exactly. When I got back from my tour of the war zone, my wife asked me how I'd felt. I told her I'd felt like Brooke Shields — and proudly unrolled the commendations I'd received.

Then it suddenly dawned on me that for the first time in my life, I had attracted institutional approval, and worse, that that approval had come from my first target all those years ago — the military establishment. Frankly, I can do without that kind of cheap irony in my life.

264

"To Garry Trudeau, for significant contributions to the morale of the United States forces deployed on Operation Desert Storm.... We are proud to induct you into our ranks as an honorary BANDIT for life."

—*Certificate of Achievement
4th Battalion 67th Armor
Kuwait City*

*A war zone keepsake from
Elvis's old unit.*

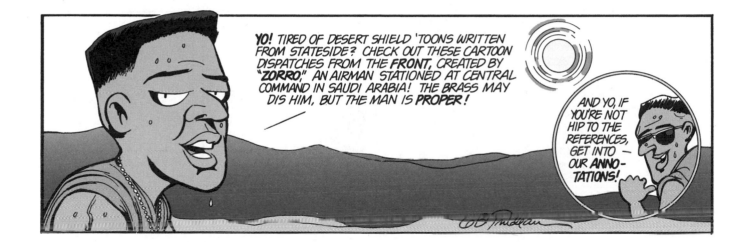

Iranian graphics were no match for Centcom's.

Mission accomplished: 1991's most critically acclaimed piece of cake.

Club Scud:
Home of the
$100
hamburger.

OKAY, WE'RE NOW LOOKING AT SOME COCKPIT FOOTAGE FROM AN OPTICALLY GUIDED MISSILE LAUNCHED FROM AN F-117A STEALTH FIGHTER...

THIS IS A CHEMICAL WEAPONS FACILITY WEST OF BAGHDAD. INTELLIGENCE HAD DISCOVERED THAT A ROOF DOOR HAD BEEN LEFT AJAR...

Beating CNN with the latest S-2 IPB's and TLAM-C BDA's. Unilaterals got benched.

AS YOU CAN SEE, THE MISSILE ACCESSES THE FACILITY, THREADS ITS WAY DOWN A STAIRWELL, THEN BACK UP A NARROW HEATING DUCT...

...PAST STARTLED IRAQI PRODUCTION MANAGERS AND INTO THE OFFICE OF THE FACILITY ADMINISTRATOR.

UNFORTUNATELY, IT CONTINUES THROUGH AN OPEN WINDOW AND EXPLODES IN A NEARBY PARKING LOT.

STILL, YA GOTTA BE IMPRESSED...

GENERAL, ARE WE WINNING THE WAR?

Don't shoot, I'm yours.
B.D. had a rocky re-entry.

THIS BETTER BE GOOD...

WHA...? I PAID $300 FOR THAT?

KUWAIT HIGH SCHOOL 1991 YEARBOOK

What a year it's been for the seniors! First, classes were suspended for the fall and winter. Most of us left for Cairo or Gstaad. Then, liberation! What a hoot! As Prince Tariq "Disco" Al-Amiri put it, "Saddam Hussein can eat my shorts!" Even with no classes, five guys got into Princeton and three into UCLA, so the year wasn't a total loss. Also, there was the senior prom -- talk about a blast! Thanks to Sheik al-Sabah for letting us use his townhouse in London, and to the whole class for showing so much spirit. Go, Scorpions!

YOUSSEF AL-MIAZ
"Al" "The Man"
Class President... Slept through the invasion... Treasurer for neighborhood resistance cell... "Grow up!"...Quote: "Down with the dens of treason and shame, as mentioned in our previous communique."

HAMED AL-MESBAH
"Ham" "Pee-Wee"
Vice Preskirnt... illegal editorial... weenie reforms ... boycotted Emir's party... working at McDonald's... "sweet spot" on a baseball... Ambition: "to move Kuwait into the 15th century."

ABDEL AL-SABAH
"Prince" "Your Majesty"
Class Treasurer... "I'm outa here!"... Christmas in Aspen... Waterbombing his bodyguard... CNN freak... Bootsie in Bahrain... Trying to grow a mustache...Gold sneaker eyelets... Polo I, II.

AHMAD SALMAN
"Stinky" "Traitor"
Class Secretary... P.L.O. donation boxes... Only guy in school who could fix the air conditioning... "Go, Intifada!"... Soccer I, II... Uncle Hussein... Missing for two months.

A LOT OF PEOPLE SAID IT COULDN'T BE DONE!

THEY SAID **NOBODY** PUTS AIR BAGS IN MINIVANS! IT'S **TOO TOUGH** TO ENGINEER!

CHRYSLER SAYS, SO **WHAT** IF EVERYBODY ELSE WANTS TO WAIT!

SOME THINGS YA WAIT FOR! PASSENGER-SIDE AIR BAGS IN MINIVANS? OKAY, YA WAIT FOR THOSE. DRIVER-SIDE AIR BAGS? **YA DON'T WAIT!**

BUT, CHAIRMAN IACOCCA — **YOU** WAITED FOR 18 YEARS! **NOBODY** IN THE INDUSTRY FOUGHT AIR BAGS HARDER! AND YOU **LED** THE CHARGE AGAINST STRUCTURAL SAFETY STANDARDS FOR MINIVANS! WHAT **GIVES** HERE?

CUT!

WHAT? WHAT? WOULDN'T A BOARD MEMBER TAKE HIM ON?

ACTORS!

66 *I see* Doonesbury *is going to do a column on why did I wait 18 years when I had the technology in my pocket. Well, that's bullshit.* **99**

—LEE IACOCCA
Chrysler Chairman

Scores of newspapers and commentators denounce a *Doonesbury* series on the treatment of Brett Kimberlin, a Federal prisoner who had made accusations about Dan Quayle and possible drug use. "The truth or falsity of Mr. Kimberlin's drug charges is not the issue," opined *The New York Times*. "What's in question is the credibility of the Justice Department's explanation for his severe discipline."

J. Edgar Williams, of Chatham County, NC, files a complaint with the Federal Election Commission against Trudeau, Trudeau's syndicate, and every newspaper carrying *Doonesbury*, contending that two strips carrying Jerry Brown's 1-800 number amounted to millions of dollars in free advertising and violated campaign finance laws. The two strips did keep Brown volunteers busy answering phones. "It was great," said Brown press secretary Ileana Wachtel. "It brought in a lot of contributions."

February 1992

When a *Doonesbury* strip encourages readers to seek Texas residency, over 45,000 Texan wannabes send in coupons from all 50 states, Canada, Brazil, Japan, and Kuwait. Texas Controller John Sharp refuses to give the names of Pennsylvania applicants to tax officials from that state, who want "to see if they had paid their state income taxes."

Mr. John Sharp
State Comptroller
Box 13528, Capitol Station
Austin, Texas 78711

Dear Mr. Sharp:
Howdy! I'd like to become a Texan. I hereby solemnly swear that it is my intention to live in Texas at some later date. (I understand there is no legal require- ment that I actually do so, and can change my mind later without tax penalty.) Please send me a certificate of residency without delay.
Sincerely,

_____
NAME

_____
MAILING ADDRESS *(BUT NOT WHERE MY HEART IS.)*

_____
CITY   STATE   ZIP

American Cancer Society takes on Mr. Butts as spokesproduct for the Great American Smokeout.

Just say yes. Prevention through irony.

WAITE A MINUT!
WAITE A MINUT!

December **1992**

Working Woman magazine names *Doonesbury's* Joanie Caucus and Lacey Davenport as among the best role models for women.

HEY, **KIDS**! EVER AMAZED BY SOME OF THE PRODUCTION VALUES IN THIS FEATURE? EVER WONDER HOW IT'S ALL DONE?

FOR INSTANCE, TAKE OUR WHITE HOUSE TABLEAU. LOOKS LIKE A COSTLY LOCATION SET-UP, RIGHT?

LOOK AGAIN! IT'S NOTHING BUT A TINY SCALE MODEL OF THE REAL THING!

THE MAGIC OF MINIATURES — A KEY ELEMENT OF BIG-TIME CARTOONING!

WELCOME TO THE WHITE HOUSE!

HEE, HEE! THAT'S "BILL CLINTON" SPEAKING! BY PUTTING WORDS IN HIS MOUTH, WE CAN OFFER TIMELY POLITICAL SATIRE!

I CAN FEEL YOUR PAIN!

OF COURSE, WHAT **REALLY** COUNTS ARE THE REGULAR CHARACTERS...

AIEE!

GB Trudeau

*Foamboard and mirrors:
Deconstructing the magic.*

Panel 1:
WE JUST GOT ANOTHER PICTURE OF ALEX FROM J.J.—IT'S PRETTY CUTE...

HOW'S EVERYONE DOING?

Panel 2:
WELL, NOT SO GREAT, ACTUALLY. MIKE STILL HASN'T FOUND A PERMANENT JOB.

Panel 3:
I'M A LITTLE WORRIED ABOUT HIM. BEING OUT OF WORK THAT LONG CAN GRIND YOU DOWN. IT CAN CHANGE YOU.

Panel 4:
HONEY? I'M GOING OUT TO DO THE SHOPLIFTING!

WE NEED MILK.

Panel 5:
OH, MIKE... YOU'RE NOT ACTUALLY DOING SUPERMARKET PULL-OUTS NOW, ARE YOU?

Panel 6:
HEY, WHAT'S WRONG WITH THAT? I'M PROUD OF THEM! SOME OF THESE SMALL JOBS ARE AMONG THE BEST WORK I'VE DONE!

Panel 7:
IT'S TRUE, MOM! DAD JUST DID A REALLY NEAT AD FOR A CHILDREN'S THEATER!

I DID?

HE DID?

Panel 8:
"LIVE SHOWS HOURLY— GIRLS! GIRLS! GIRLS!"

UM...RIGHT! AND THOSE LADIES ARE THEIR MOMMIES!

ON THEIR WAY TO THE BEACH.

Panel 9:
MOM, IT'S JUST GETTING WORSE. IT'S LIKE MIKE HAS PUT HIS INTEGRITY IN A LITTLE BOX AND STORED IT AWAY...

Panel 10:
NOW, DEAR, MIKE'S JUST TRYING TO SUPPORT HIS FAMILY...

I KNOW, BUT IT'S LIKE HE'LL TAKE ANY JOB NOW—NO MATTER **WHO** THE CLIENT!

Panel 11:
NOW, NOW, THAT DOESN'T SOUND LIKE MIKE...

WHO'S THAT ON THE PHONE?

Panel 12:
SOME TERRORIST GROUP. THEY NEED A LEAFLET DONE.

BY WHEN?

Post rock bottom. Downsizing in the '90s.

293

August *1993*

A Santa Barbara skateboard shop gets in trouble with a customer's mother for selling a pirated "Mr. Butts" skateboard. Owner of the shop Michael Magne defends himself: "It's not that big a deal. It's a joke. There's no other way to take it unless you're a moron." He urges a reporter, "Make us look like we're straight from hell because that's the best kind of press. The kids are going to look at us like Gods."

His muscles, his pickup named Harry, his love of poetry, his muscles, his camera named Travis, his love of vegetables, his last-of-the-breed cowboy-shaman ways.

YOU COULD GET A FRESH START! RE-TRAIN!

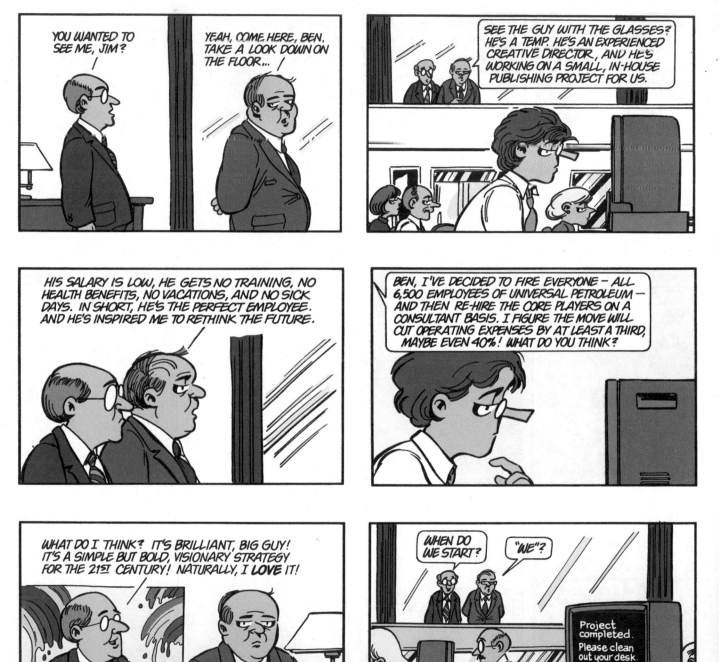

YOU WANTED TO SEE ME, JIM?

YEAH, COME HERE, BEN, TAKE A LOOK DOWN ON THE FLOOR...

SEE THE GUY WITH THE GLASSES? HE'S A TEMP. HE'S AN EXPERIENCED CREATIVE DIRECTOR, AND HE'S WORKING ON A SMALL, IN-HOUSE PUBLISHING PROJECT FOR US.

HIS SALARY IS LOW, HE GETS NO TRAINING, NO HEALTH BENEFITS, NO VACATIONS, AND NO SICK DAYS. IN SHORT, HE'S THE PERFECT EMPLOYEE. AND HE'S INSPIRED ME TO RETHINK THE FUTURE.

BEN, I'VE DECIDED TO FIRE EVERYONE — ALL 6,500 EMPLOYEES OF UNIVERSAL PETROLEUM — AND THEN RE-HIRE THE CORE PLAYERS ON A CONSULTANT BASIS. I FIGURE THE MOVE WILL CUT OPERATING EXPENSES BY AT LEAST A THIRD, MAYBE EVEN 40%! WHAT DO YOU THINK?

WHAT DO I THINK? IT'S BRILLIANT, BIG GUY! IT'S A SIMPLE BUT BOLD, VISIONARY STRATEGY FOR THE 21ST CENTURY! NATURALLY, I LOVE IT!

WHEN DO WE START?

"WE"?

Project completed. Please clean out your desk.

©B Trudeau

A one o'clock with Bdippl
at Cafe Fwiblob.

For Mark, a shiny, brand-new
sexual orientation.

Kind of falls into place, doesn't it?

—SEN. GEORGE MITCHELL

HE'S LYING RIGHT NOW, ISN'T HE?

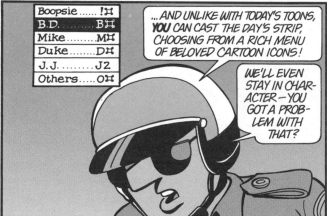

...AND FINALLY, TO PARENTS HERE TODAY, A BIT OF ADVICE: SUFFER YOUR CHILDREN GLADLY.

IF THEY DO NOT MAKE THEIR WAY OUT INTO THE WORLD IMMEDIATELY, IT IS BECAUSE THE WORLD HAS BECOME SUCH A FORBIDDING PLACE IN THESE TIMES...

NEVER HAS A CLASS GRADUATED INTO SUCH AN UNCERTAIN AND BLEAK ECONOMIC ENVIRONMENT...

HOW BLEAK? WELL, THIS YEAR ONLY A SINGLE COMPANY RECRUITED ON CAMPUS, DOWN FROM TWO LAST YEAR!

WE ARE, OF COURSE, DEEPLY GRATEFUL TO THE REMAINING EMPLOYER FOR ITS COMMITMENT TO OUR FINE GRADUATES...

GAP! GAP! GAP! GAP!

WOOF! WOOF! WOOF!

...BUT LOSING McDONALD'S WAS A BLOW.

311

From Woodstock to Woodstock:
What a long, strange strip it's been.

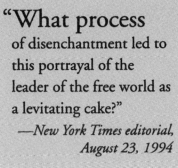

"Rep. Thomas Bliley said he joked with incoming House Speaker Newt Gingrich, R-Ga., about their appearances in *Doonesbury*. According to Bliley, Gingrich said: 'That shows just how far we've come as Republicans, that they would take up space with both of us in one week's time!'"

—*Richmond Times Dispatch*, December 9, 1994

OKAY, WHAT *REALLY* HAPPENED, SON? WERE YOU MUGGED?

TRY TO
UNDER-
STAND—
THIS WAS
ARKANSAS.

YOU WANTED TO SEE ME, SIR?

YES, LLOYD, I WANTED TO TALK TO YOU ABOUT THAT DAMN VIDEO...

WHAT VIDEO IS THAT, SIR?

THE TAPE THAT JERRY FALWELL HAS BEEN PEDDLING ON HIS SHOW WITH PHIL CRANE'S ENDORSEMENT.

I'M AFRAID I HAVEN'T SEEN IT, SIR.

WELL, YOU SHOULD! IT ACCUSES ME OF SEXUAL HARASSMENT, OF COCAINE ADDICTION, OF RUNNING A MONEY-LAUNDERING OPERATION FOR A DRUG RING...

... AND OF ORDERING THE BEATINGS AND MURDERS OF SEVERAL POLITICAL OPPONENTS! CAN YOU BELIEVE IT? FALWELL AND CRANE ARE ACCUSING ME OF **MURDER**!

THAT'S ASTONISHING, SIR. IT'D BE IN-CREDIBLY VILE IF IT WEREN'T SO LUDICROUS!

WELL, EXACTLY. WHAT DO YOU THINK I SHOULD DO?

UM... IGNORE IT?

REALLY? I WAS THINKING OF A COVER-UP.

THIS IS ROLAND HEDLEY. IN THE MONTHS AHEAD, THIS FINE FEATURE WILL BE SWITCHING TO AN ALL-O.J. FORMAT! I'LL BE BREAKING THE BIG STORIES...

...WHILE I HANDLE ANALYSIS OF THE LARGER SOCIAL ISSUES RAISED!

TO SUPPLEMENT THE PRESS COVERAGE, I'LL BE OFFERING A FIRST-HAND ACCOUNT FROM THE JURY BOX...

...AS WILL I!

...BOTH OF WHOM ARE REPPED BY YOURS TRULY, AGENT TO A HOT LINE-UP OF MAJOR O.J. PLAYERS!

...INCLUDING ME, A FORMER PRO ATHLETE WITH PLENTY OF IN-SIGHT INTO THE VIOLENT UNDERSIDE OF SPORTS!

...AND ME, BOTH PEACE OFFICER AND AFRICAN AMERICAN! I'LL BE PROVIDING PUNGENT COMMENTARY ON THE RACIAL DIMENSIONS OF O.J.'S TRIAL RIGHT UP TO HIS ACQUITTAL!

...WHILE I HANDLE COLOR DUTIES! AS A NATIVE CALI-FORNIAN, I'LL MAKE SENSE OF THE LOCAL ZEITGEIST— AND TRANSLATE THE TRIAL TESTIMONY OF FELLOW DUDE "KATO" KAELIN!

SO FOR WALL-TO-WALL O.J. COVERAGE...

...THINK TEAM DOONESBURY!

WE'RE THE O.J. SPECIALISTS!

GB Trudeau

"BOYS TOWN"?

Q .... We're running out of book. Whither the comics?

A .... If comics were important to a pre-literate America, they're absolutely indispensible to a post-literate one. When people tell me they keep up with the news through *Doonesbury*, I tremble for the republic, but the truth is, everyone has time for the comics. They get under people's skin. My favorite readers are the sort who write to complain that I've been wrong every day for the last 20 years. That's a long time to chew sandpaper, but you'd be surprised how many people do it.

Kate: IMHO, Chakotay is the most compelling First Officer since Spock.

Mike: Same with Janeway and Kirk.

TAP! TAP!

Cliff: Anyone catch the quarter singularity repeat last night?

Mike: Yeah, I did. Sick of the villain being another spatial phenomenon.

TAP! TAP!

Ted: I agree. Let Trek be Trek. More Klingons!

Cliff: Right on, Ted. Voyager hasn't cut it, characterwise, since episode six, BTW.

Kate: 'Bye, guys. Gotta go to work.

Mike: Work?

TAP! TAP!

OH, NO...

MOMMY! DADDY STAYED UP ALL NIGHT AGAIN!

Mike: Isn't Capt. Janeway's expertise in temporal mechanics?

July 8 1995

The University of California releases documents that allegedly claim that tobacco giant Brown & Williamson hid knowledge of the addictive properties of nicotine. The documents had been sent to UC–San Francisco Professor Stanton Glantz. The only return address listed was "Mr. Butts."

Lyndon Johnson once said that it was better to have would-be critics inside the tent pissing out than outside pissing in. Where do you stand on co-option?

A

When I first started drawing President Clinton as a waffle, the AP ran a story about how I had jeopardized my standing with the Adminstration, and that I was unlikely to be asked to any more White House dinners. When a friend of mine expressed surprise that I had *ever* been invited by the Clintons to dinner, I replied that I hadn't — that, in fact, if I had been, this whole nasty business with the waffle could have been avoided.

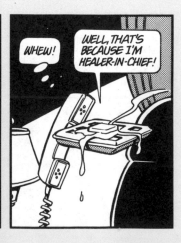

— SEN. PHIL GRAMM
on his treatment in Doonesbury

March 24 **1995**

Senators John McCain and Bob Kerrey rise on the Senate floor to denounce Trudeau for his strip on Bob Dole's campaign strategy to exploit his war record. Says McCain: "Suffice it to say that I hold him in utter contempt."

YOU KNOW, IF VOTERS HAVE SENT US ONE MESSAGE LOUD AND CLEAR...

...IT'S THAT THEY'RE TIRED OF GOVERNMENT INSPECTORS TELLING THEM WHAT TO EAT, DRINK AND BREATHE!

TAKE SPOILED MEAT— IT COSTS US 4,000 LIVES, 5 MILLION ILL-NESSES AND OVER $3 BILLION IN MEDI-CAL EXPENSES YEARLY.

BUT DOES THAT JUSTI-FY THE HORRIFIC REG-ULATORY BURDEN ON THE MEAT INDUSTRY? COULDN'T WE LIVE WITH 8,000 DEATHS? OR 12,000?

AMERICANS ARE **CRYING OUT** FOR COST-BENEFIT RATIOS THAT MAKE SENSE TO BUS-INESS! IF I'M ELECT-ED, THEY'LL GET 'EM!

BOB DOLE FOR PRESIDENT.

BECAUSE WE ALL HAVE TO DIE OF SOME-THING.

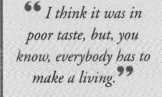

66 *I think it was in poor taste, but, you know, everybody has to make a living.* 99

— BOB DOLE

PHOTOGRAPHY CREDITS

Matthew Klein: 11, 19, 33, 47, 58, 77, 78, 82, 83, 100, 101, 107, 123, 135, 159, 171, 183, 187, 212, 244, 256, 258, 261, 264, 267, 268, 270, 283, 289, 293, 299. **FPG:** 27, Carson Baldwin; 84, Oscar Nelder; 96, Newsworld/New York Tribune; 104, Newsworld/New York Tribune; 109, Paul Kern; 113, FPG Int'l; 137, Isaiah Karlinsky; 167, Peter Borsari; 173, Mike Valeri; 175, Laurence Agron; 176, Mark Reinstein; 185, Arthur D'Amario III; 196, The News World; 215, Mark Reinstein; 229, Laurence Agron; 235, Laurence Agron; 273, Joe Crachiola; 275, Chris Mooney; 276, Peter Borsari; 288, Mark Reinstein; 305, Mark Reinstein; 311, Mark Reinstein; 329, Mark Reinstein. **Black Star:** 49, Dennis Brack; 73, Dennis Brack; 117, Dennis Brack; 121, Dennis Brack; 147, Dennis Brack; 222, Bill Foley; 231, Lisa Quinones; 249, Rick Friedman; 280, Rick Friedman; 331, Rick Friedman. **AP/Wide World Photos:** 24, 37, 64, 66, 129, 156, 225, 296, 304. **Vireo:** 209, J.H. Dick (Academy of Natural Sciences). **Courtesy of:** 141, *The Recorder*, Greenfield, MA; 164, John Leonard; 205, George Will; 289, White House model from *Mouse House: 5 Easy-To-Build Homes For Your Computer Mouse* by Jim Becker, Andy Mayer and Doug Mayer, illustrations by Dick Witt and Bob Greisen, Penguin Books, 1995. **With permission:** 22, *Chicago Tribune*; 97, *San Francisco Examiner* photo, John Gorman; 177, *Times-Advocate*, Escondido, Ca.